# Global Cities

# NEW YORK

Sally Garrington
photographs by Chris Fairclough

Evans

Published by
Evans Brothers Limited,
Part of the Evans Publishing Group,
2A Portman Mansions
Chiltern Street
London WIU 6NR

VISIT OUR WEBSITE
www.evansbooks.co.uk

First published 2006
© copyright Evans Brothers Limited

British Library Cataloguing in Publication Data

Garrington, Sally
New York. - (Global cities)
1.New York (N.Y.) - Juvenile literature
I.Title
974.7'1044

ISBN-10: 0237531003
13-digit ISBN (from 1 January 2007) 9780237 531003

Designer: Robert Walster, Big Blu Design
Maps and graphics by Martin Darlinson
All photographs are by Chris Fairclough except:
Corbis p. 12 top, p. 45 top right, p.50, p. 51, p. 55 top.

easi-er

Series concept and project management EASI –
Educational Resourcing
(info@easi-er.co.uk)

# Contents

# Living in an urban world

Sometime in 2007 the world's population will, for the first time in history, become more urban than rural. An estimated 3.3 billion people will find themselves living in towns and cities like New York, and for many, the experience of urban living will be relatively new. For example, in China, the world's most populous country, the number of people living in urban areas increased from 196 million in 1980 to over 536 million by 2005.

## The urban challenge...

This staggering rate of urbanisation (the process by which a country's population becomes concentrated into towns and cities), is being repeated across much of the world and presents the world with a complex set of challenges for the 21st century. Many of these challenges are local, like the provision of clean water for expanding urban populations, but others are global in scale. In 2003 an outbreak of the highly contagious SARS disease demonstrated this as it spread rapidly among the populations of well-connected cities across the globe. The pollution generated by urban areas is also a global concern, particularly as urban residents tend to generate more than their rural counterparts.

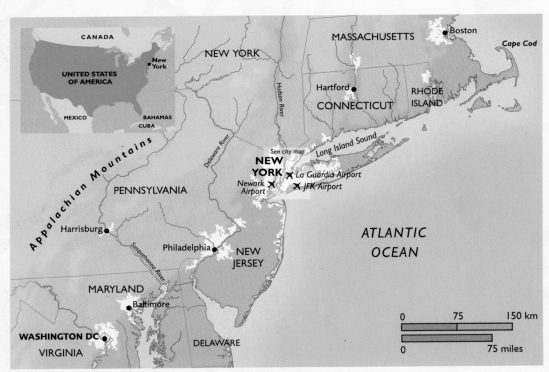

▲ New York in relation to the cities and states of the northeastern USA.

# ... and opportunity!

Urban centres, and particularly major cities like New York, also provide great opportunities for improving life at both a local and global scale. Cities concentrate people and allow for efficient forms of mass transport like subway or light rail networks. Services too, such as waste collection, recycling, education and health can all function more efficiently in a city.

Cities are centres of learning and often the birthplace of new ideas, from innovations in science and technology to new ways of day-to-day living. Cities also provide a platform for the celebration of arts and culture and, as their populations become more multicultural – such celebrations are increasingly global in their reach.

▼ Manhattan, the heart of New York, is a world centre of business, finance and culture.

# The boroughs

New York is made up of five boroughs: Manhattan, Brooklyn, Queens, the Bronx and Staten Island. The most famous of these is the island borough of Manhattan, where most of the popular tourist sites are located. The Bronx is found to the north of Manhattan across the Harlem River, on the mainland. Queens and Brooklyn are at the western end of Long Island – Queens to the north and Brooklyn to the south. Finally, Staten Island is located south of Manhattan Island opposite south Brooklyn. Beyond these boroughs is Greater New York, which includes part of the states of New York, New Jersey and Connecticut.

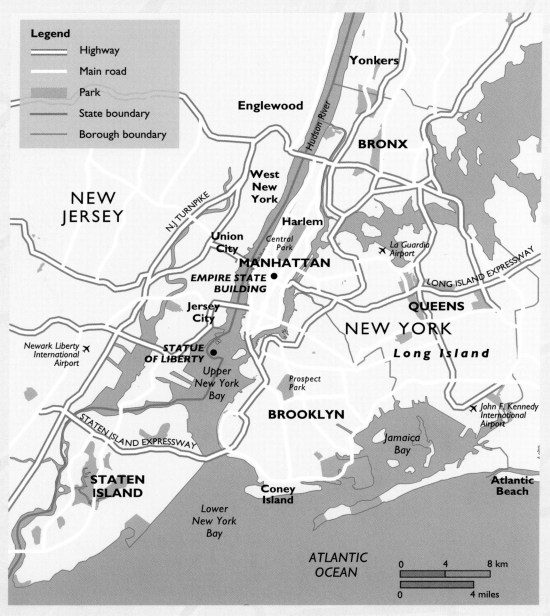

Legend

- Highway
- Main road
- Park
- State boundary
- Borough boundary

Yonkers

Englewood

Hudson River

BRONX

West New York

NEW JERSEY

NJ TURNPIKE

Harlem

Central Park

La Guardia Airport

Union City

MANHATTAN

EMPIRE STATE BUILDING

LONG ISLAND EXPRESSWAY

Jersey City

QUEENS

NEW YORK

Long Island

Newark Liberty International Airport

STATUE OF LIBERTY

Upper New York Bay

Prospect Park

John F. Kennedy International Airport

STATEN ISLAND EXPRESSWAY

BROOKLYN

Jamaica Bay

STATEN ISLAND

Lower New York Bay

Coney Island

Atlantic Beach

ATLANTIC OCEAN

0   4   8 km

0   4 miles

# Gateway to America

New York was, and is still, regarded by many as the main entry point to the USA. The Statue of Liberty stands in New York harbour to remind people that the USA is a country of immigrants. Many have not ventured far from where they or their parents landed in New York harbour. The wide diversity of neighbourhoods within the city reflects its many different races and cultures. In the city there are significant communities of Italians, Koreans, Chinese and Russians, to name but a few. This mix of peoples creates the feeling of vibrancy in the city as they contribute their foods, dress style and customs.

# A working city

New York's importance began as a trading port. This attracted service industries like banking and insurance, and was the beginning of New York's important financial industry. The Financial District around Wall Street is one of the most important in the world. Its status as a hub for international trade has led many international businesses and organisations to establish headquarters in New York. The city is also the global headquarters for the United Nations.

▲ The Statue of Liberty, given by the French nation in 1886, is seen around the world as a symbol of freedom.

# A city of many attractions

Visitors come to New York for many reasons. Some arrive on business, some for shopping and others for the cultural attractions – to experience its special mix of history and culture. It has many museums and galleries, including the Guggenheim Museum on Fifth Avenue and the National Museum of the American Indian. There are green spaces such as Central Park where people can relax. Boat tours and ferries ply the East and Hudson Rivers, giving a completely different view of the city from the water. There are many street parades and celebrations representing the huge cultural diversity of the city's population.

◀ The Brooklyn Bridge, completed in 1883, is regarded as one of the industrial wonders of the world.

11

# The history of New York

Native Americans were living on Manhattan Island 11,000 years before Europeans came to America. The island was called Manahatouh, which means a place for gathering wood for bows. There was an ancient path that crossed the island diagonally, which is now the route taken by Broadway. On the City Seal is a representation of the original occupiers of Manhattan Island, standing to the right of the central shield.

▲ The City Seal includes several elements of the city's history, such as the beavers representing the early fur trade, and was used from the seventeenth century. The latin inscription says, 'Seal of the City of New York'.

◀ Liberty Island, home to the Statue of Liberty, is a popular destination for tourists visiting New York.

## The coming of the Europeans

The first Europeans to settle the area were the Dutch, who called the whole region New Netherlands and the new settlement New Amsterdam. In the shield on the City Seal which is still used today there are sails of a Dutch windmill showing the Dutch origins of the city. Flour and beaver pelts were two important early exports. As the main markets for these products were in Europe a large merchant fleet was soon established in the port, and sailors' families formed a large part of the population. In 1664 the city was taken over by the British and renamed New York.

# The growing city

In 1781 the American War of Independence gave the colonies of North America independence from Great Britain. In that year the population of New York City was 33,000. The chance of jobs and a better life attracted people from within America and from countries overseas as distant as Scotland, Ireland and Germany. The nineteenth century was a period of rapid urbanisation as housing had to be built for these new Americans. By 1830 the population had risen to 250,000. In 1825 New York was linked to the Great Lakes and the interior of the United States by the building of the Erie Canal, which linked with the Hudson River. More trade was then sent through New York's port, creating more jobs and attracting even more people. By 1850 the population was 515,547, making New York the second largest city in the world.

By the beginning of the twentieth century the first skyscrapers were being built, which were to give New York its distinctive skyline. Rapid urbanisation continued and by 1930 the population was seven million. Just before this date, in 1929, there was a huge financial disaster when the stock market on Wall Street (at the southern end of Manhattan) crashed. Many firms went out of business and millions of people lost all of their money. This was the start of a period known as the Great Depression. Huge numbers of people were left unemployed across America and much of the world. The Depression only ended with the start of World War Two in Europe, in 1939.

▶ The 91 m-high Flatiron building was the tallest building in the world when it was built in 1902. Its steel frame construction and the invention of mechanical lifts made its height possible.

# The Forties and Fifties

After the war the headquarters of the new United Nations organisation was established in New York in 1946, and the city's importance as a financial centre grew as the giant US economy expanded. During the 1940s and 1950s the middle classes moved further into suburbia to escape the problems associated with city living – high levels of crime, pollution and poor city services. At the same time manufacturing industry was slowing and service industries did not immediately replace it. The television and film industry moved to Los Angeles, California. The city began to decline.

▼ Moving to the outer boroughs, such as here on Staten Island, New Yorkers could enjoy more space.

# The Sixties and Seventies

These were unhappy years for New York. Racial tensions exploded into riots in Harlem, caused largely by poor living conditions and unemployment during hot summers. City services were poorly run and maintained and the middle classes continued to leave the city's central areas. This slow decay reached its lowest point in 1975 when the city was on the verge

of bankruptcy. New York was only saved with a huge loan from the US government. The completion of the Twin Towers of the World Trade Center in the mid-70s marked the emergence of a healthier economy.

▼ The Twin Towers of the World Trade Center became a symbol of the rebirth of the city. They were destroyed by terrorists in 2001.

## Into the 21st century

The 1980s began well for New York —
businesses flourished and property prices
rose rapidly, but this period of growth
ended with another stock market crash in
1987. This crash was a serious setback for
the city's financial businesses. After a slow
recovery the 1990s were marked by the
policies of the administration of Mayor
Rudolph Giuliani. He took a no-nonsense
stand on crime and worked to clean up
many areas of the city. On September 11th
2001 the twin towers of the World Trade
Center were destroyed by terrorists flying
two aeroplanes into them. For a while
there was a reduction in both business
transactions and tourism. On July 4th 2004
the cornerstone was laid of the Freedom
Tower that is to replace the Twin Towers
and reach the same height within the
Manhattan skyline. Since then the city's
economy has recovered, and although the
gap between rich and poor seems to be

▲ The site of the Twin Towers is now known as
Ground Zero. Work has started on a replacement
tower, designed by the architect Daniel Liebeskind.

widening, the quality of life for the
majority of New Yorkers is improving
overall. Many former industrial areas are
being redeveloped as new housing, green
space or business locations and New York
is looking to provide all of its inhabitants
with the means to enjoy a city life.

## CASE STUDY

## Firefighter
## Kevin Erdman

Kevin has been a firefighter for over 20
years and lost five friends in the terrorist
attack of September 11th 2001. He wants
to see the Twin Towers site developed as a
memorial to those who died. "New York
City has always been a difficult city to fight
fires in – any modern city with this many
high-rise buildings and skyscrapers has to
be hard: ladders are only so long! So our
challenge as firefighters has to be one of
prevention and not cure. No fire service
could have better dealt with the tragedy
of 9/11. We did our best and lost some of
the best doing our job but we saved lives,
lots of lives."

# The people of New York

Early European settlement of the city of New York began with the Dutch and the English, but these nationalities were soon to be joined by people from many other countries. New York's position as the premier port for the USA meant it was the main point of entry for most migrants up until the latter part of the twentieth century. Many immigrants settled in the city through which they entered the country.

▲ There is a very broad range of ethnic backgrounds among New Yorkers – including European, Afro-Caribbean and Asian.

Up until the nineteenth century most immigrants were from western and northern Europe. In the 1840s there was a huge surge in Irish immigration, driven from Ireland by the impact of the severe famines caused by the failure of the potato crop. The nineteenth century also saw large numbers of Jews migrating to avoid persecution in eastern Europe and Russia.

From 1870 to 1930 Italians also formed an important immigrant group. By 1890 42 per cent of the population of New York City was European-born.

All of these peoples crowded into the city, often living in very cramped and unhealthy conditions, frequently with a family of six or seven living in one room. The pressure caused by a continuous flow of people meant that the city grew outwards and those with some money left the crowded areas on Manhattan Island and moved to the new suburbs of Brooklyn, Queens and the Bronx. Many immigrants to New York and America came through the Ellis Island Immigration Station (opened in 1892) – it is estimated that before it closed in 1954, 12 million people had passed through. On arrival immigrants were given health checks and any who had infectious diseases were sent back to their country of origin.

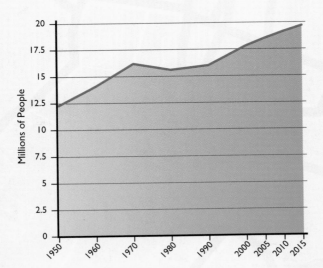

◄ The population growth of the Greater New York area from 1950 onwards.

# Expansion

Today the city continues to grow as it attracts migrants from abroad. New migrants are now more likely to come from Asia than Europe. Over a third of all New Yorkers are now first generation immigrants, a figure unmatched since the last great wave of immigration between 1880 and 1920. Some will find well-paid positions, but most new migrants will find jobs in the low income bracket. New York also attracts people from within the USA, as it offers a stimulating environment for people with new ideas in many different fields, from technology to the arts. However, the growth of the city has led to problems with transport links, housing, air and noise pollution, and problems with water supply and waste disposal.

▲ Many African Americans moved to New York from the southern states after the Civil War in search of the chance for a better life.

▲ Traffic congestion is a major problem for the city, as more and more vehicles try to use an outdated road system.

**17**

# The neighbourhoods

People refer to New York as a city of neighbourhoods – there are many distinctive areas within the city. These alter according to the ethnic background and culture of the residents. As each group of migrants entered the city they tended to look for people who were from the same culture and spoke the same language. They needed someone who could explain what was expected of them as new citizens in the city, where they could find familiar foods and how they could get employment.

There is a Little Italy, the Jewish Quarter, Little India and a Little Korea. The Jewish area was originally situated around the Lower East Side and there are still Jewish businesses and synagogues in this area. Today many of the Jews have moved out to more spacious neighbourhoods in Brooklyn and their place has been taken by the expansion of Chinatown. Chinatown is an old and distinctive district with its specialised shops, markets, restaurants and temples.

▼ In the Jewish Quarter the distinctive dress of the Jewish males adds to the character of the area.

### Racial structure of the boroughs by percentage

| Borough | White | Hispanic | Black | Asian | Other |
|---|---|---|---|---|---|
| Bronx | 14.5 | 48.4 | 31.2 | 2.9 | 3 |
| Brooklyn | 34.7 | 19.8 | 34.4 | 7.5 | 3.6 |
| Manhattan | 45.8 | 27.2 | 15.3 | 9.4 | 2.3 |
| Queens | 32.9 | 25 | 19 | 17.5 | 5.6 |
| Staten Island | 71.3 | 12.1 | 8.9 | 5.6 | 2.1 |

Source: Adapted from US Census 2000

# Harlem

Harlem stretches north from the top of Central Park up to 140th Street and is the most important African American residential district in New York. Originally an area of country estates, it was developed for the middle classes after the coming of the subway at the start of the twentieth century. However, not enough people were willing to move out that far and so the houses were sub-divided and let to poorer African Americans.

Harlem developed a distinctive black culture with jazz and blues clubs, soul food restaurants and shops. Lack of maintenance of much of the housing, poor schools and high crime and unemployment rates led to the area becoming run down. By the end of the 1970s there had been a 30 per cent decline in the population as families left for other suburbs. Today, with its desirable brownstone houses and easy access to central New York, Harlem is attracting a wide range of people of all ethnic backgrounds. African Americans still make up over three quarters of the population. Young professionals are buying up the old

▲ Traditional brownstone houses in Harlem.

houses and improving the interiors (the exteriors are protected by law). The money these new residents bring into the area boosts the local economy, but also means that the character of the area is changing for the residents brought up there.

## CASE STUDY

## Harlem resident – Elenor Watson

Elenor originally came from Belize and has lived in Harlem for ten years. She is a single mother of two teenage boys and works as a street cleaner. "Harlem used to be thought of as a 'black only' suburb but now it's becoming a very trendy place to live. Young professionals from lower Manhattan are buying up all the houses and putting security gates on them. The area isn't as friendly now and people no longer sit on the steps to talk about their day. Developers want to buy up where I live and fill it with city types, but I like it here."

▲ A graduate class from a language school celebrates finishing their course.

# The newest New Yorkers

In 2000 2.9 million people or 36 per cent of the population of the city of New York were foreign-born. Nearly a quarter of the foreign-born were from the continent of Asia and nearly a third were from Latin America. In 1970 two thirds of the foreign-born residents were from Europe but twenty years later, the largest source country was the Dominican Republic in the Caribbean – 369,000 migrants arrived during the 1990s. China provided 262,000 migrants during the same period. Without immigrants New York would be losing its population – from 1990 to 2000 475,000 people left the city for other states in the USA. During the same period 339,000 foreign immigrants entered the city, providing a stable population base. As the new immigrants tend to be in the younger age groups, mainly 24-35, they

are also at the age when they have children, so raising the city's birthrate and maintaining the population level.

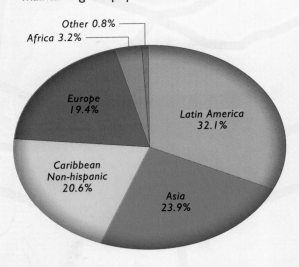

▲ Origin of recent immigrants to New York (%)

20

# Settling in

Of the new migrants coming to the city, 69 per cent settled in the largely residential areas of Queens and Brooklyn. The immigrants from the Dominican Republic tended however to settle on the west side of the Bronx where there is a well established neighbourhood of Dominicans. As immigrant groups are attracted to areas where there are already people from their cultures it has meant that many ethnic residential neighbourhoods are growing outwards.

Immigrants are needed by the city of New York to work in many areas but are found mainly in the manufacturing, construction and service industries. Those that settle fastest tend to be those who already have some knowledge of English. For those who have not there are many free courses where immigrants are encouraged to learn English as part of their commitment to citizenship in their new country. Many schools in New York run special classes for children of immigrants who have come to the USA without any English skills and give them intensive language teaching. Some schools specialise in teaching children who have never been to school in any country. They teach them in a bilingual environment to encourage learning as well as language skills.

Within the city there are many voluntary organisations which help new immigrants to find accommodation and hopefully employment. There is some government help, especially for those who are seeking asylum from persecution in their own countries.

## CASE STUDY

## Phyllis Berman

Phyllis is a director of the Riverside Language Program in New York, an institution that runs free intensive English courses for new migrants to the city. Sixty per cent of students come with no or very little English. They attend the course for six weeks and then sit an oral English examination. The origins of the students are constantly changing. "At present a third of our students are from Russia, a third from Latin American countries and the remainder are from the rest of the world. At a recent registration for new students we saw people who spoke Russian, Albanian, Romanian, Polish, Bosnian, French, Spanish, Portuguese, Chinese, Japanese, Korean, Tibetan, Italian, German, Hebrew, Arabic and some tribal languages!"

◀ Working in her office in the Upper West Side, Phyllis Berman has been overseeing English language courses for new immigrants for 26 years.

# Living in the city

New York is a city of contrasts. The noise and congestion of traffic on Fifth Avenue gives way within a block or two to the calm oasis of greenery that is Central Park. There are busy waterfronts in Brooklyn and Manhattan close to theatrical and cultural venues. Designer shops are found in central Manhattan and yet not too far away are shops selling ancient Chinese herbal remedies and oriental foods.

## Urbanisation

Manhattan is the heart of the city, but it is an island and space is restricted. Even in the nineteenth century tall, narrow houses were built to make the most of the space on Manhattan Island. Early blocks of flats called tenement blocks were built in the poorer areas. In the nineteenth century these were very crowded, poorly ventilated and were often areas where crime flourished. One such area, in today's Chelsea and the Garment District, was known as Hell's Kitchen, where many criminal gangs existed. On the very expensive central land the skyscraper was developed. In 1902 the 91 m-high Flatiron building was built (see p. 13); so tall that people thought it would fall over. This compares with the now destroyed World Trade Center, completed in 1977 and 411 m . The further out from Manhattan you travel, the more residential housing there is and the more likely it is to be low rise.

▲ Skyscraper offices and homes make the most of small plots of expensive land in the centre of the city.

## Wealth and poverty

Whilst the USA is the richest country in the world there are still poor people living there, but even the poor are relatively well off when compared to standards of living around the world. Housing developments (usually blocks of flats) for those on low income are often called 'projects'. Many poor families have to depend on money from the city in order to live. In 2002 nearly half a million people were receiving public assistance, but in New York, if people are fit they have to work for some of their welfare payments under a scheme called "Workfare". The aim is to give them the experience of working as well as some training that can help them to find a job.

▼ Large tower blocks known as 'projects' are home to many of the city's poorer residents.

# Health

Americans need to have private medical insurance to cover medical bills when they fall ill. The poorest families cannot afford this but have basic medical cover through a government scheme called Medicaid. If someone has a good job they will often have family medical insurance as part of their earnings. They are more likely to be able to access the very high quality private hospitals in the city too.

Poor north west area of Queens contrasted with wealthy Upper East side Manhattan.
(2002 City Planning Department)

|  | Queens | Manhattan |
| --- | --- | --- |
| Birth Rate (per 1000) | 9.9 | 12.8 |
| Death Rate(per 1000) | 7.4 | 6.6 |
| Infant Mortality | 2.5 | 2.2 |
| % on Medicaid | 19.5 | 4.5 |
| % White/non Hispanic | 41 | 83 |
| % Asian | 36 | 6 |
| % Hispanic | 17 | 6 |
| % Population less than 18 years | 20 | 12 |
| % Unemployed | 5.3 | 3.7 |
| % Single family dwellings | 34 | 5 |
| % Multi-Family Dwellings | 10 | 35 |
| Average Income | $46,294 | $87,428 |

# Education

In New York, school officially begins at age six – before that many children attend day care centres or kindergarten (nursery school). The school population reflects the mix of races and cultures in the city and many primary schools will have children from Caribbean, Asian, European and Hispanic origins. In New York City there are some schools that work particularly with the children of newly arrived immigrants, such as the Liberty School in Manhattan. It provides a high school environment for non-English speaking immigrants, teaching English to the students while offering cultural and artistic activities in their first languages such as Chinese, Spanish and Polish. Some high schools are specialist academies which have a curriculum that focuses on one area, such as performing arts, science or mathematics.

Some New York schools have had severe problems with violence and weapon carrying. However the number of violent incidents has fallen since the early nineties. School security has been significantly tightened – anyone found carrying a weapon in school is instantly expelled. Security guards armed with metal detectors operate at some school entrances to check students for weapons as they arrive.

New York is home to several universities – three are among the world's elite institutions: New York University (NYU), Cornell and Columbia.

▼ The Library forms a focal point within the main courtyard of Columbia University.

# Shopping

Shopping is an important activity for both residents and visitors and there is a huge range of outlets within the city. Fifth Avenue is home to many shops selling expensive clothes and accessories. Another important shopping area is the Rockefeller Centre in the Theatre District. Today it has many shops, offices and entertainment venues, as well as gardens to walk in. Bloomingdale's and Macy's are both famous department stores – Macy's is the largest in the world, taking over a whole city block, where you can buy anything from a potato peeler to jewellery.

Small grocery shops and supermarkets are common, with many providing items for particular ethnic neighbourhoods. In Grand Street there is a Chinese market which sells live seafood as well as Chinese vegetables. There are also the 'green markets' where the farmers from New York State come in to sell fresh fruit and vegetables and other produce such as honey. These are very popular with local residents as the food is so fresh and often organically-produced.

▲ The clothes in this Jewish dress shop are likely to have been made locally within the garment district of New York.

▶ Macy's is one of several very large department stores in New York.

## Hot and cold

New York has huge contrasts in its climate. Its residents need to use air conditioning units in the summer to cope with hot and humid conditions, yet must use central heating to cope with freezing winter temperatures. The city structure of concrete, stone and asphalt holds heat and the high buildings deflect winds, so the city temperature is usually a few degrees warmer than the surrounding countryside. Extreme weather events can still bring the city to a standstill. In February 2006 a storm caused a 68-cm blanket of snow. All flights from the three airports were cancelled. Temperatures dropped to -15°C and many schools and offices were closed.

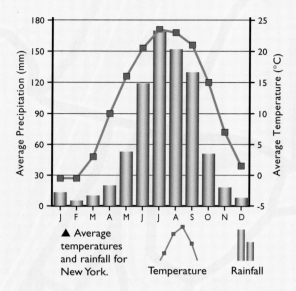

▲ Average temperatures and rainfall for New York.

Temperature    Rainfall

## Noise, pests and rubbish

Noise is the number one complaint to the city's Citizen's Complaint Hotline. New York is one of the noisiest cities in the world – the noise comes from loud music, car alarms, traffic, the constant road works and aircraft, but the main offenders are noisy neighbours, a problem especially hard to escape in Manhattan, where people live in very close proximity to one another. New York produces over 11,000 tonnes of rubbish every day. Apart from the problem of getting rid of it there is the problem of the pests that the stored rubbish attracts, especially rats. Pest control officers are continually working to get rid of infestations and encourage people to store their waste in rodent-proof containers. As well as rats, many residents constantly have to battle with cockroaches.

◄ Freezing winters are followed by sweltering summers. These children cool down in a fountain in a neighbourhood park.

# Homelessness

Like many cities, New York has many thousand homeless people. Some are homeless because they have lost their job or because they are recent immigrants. Other people are homeless because of problems with drugs or alcohol. In early March 2005 there were nearly 36,000 homeless people, including children, in emergency accommodation.

# Crime

The New York City's Police Department (NYPD) has the difficult job of policing this vast and multicultural city. It has foot, car and mounted police patrols and in June 2005 had about 35,000 officers. Since 1993 the number and severity of crime incidents has reduced and the Department is looking to prevent crime from happening rather than dealing with the situation after the

▲ Many homeless people can be seen on the streets.

event. The Crime Prevention Section of the NYPD carries out security surveys for residents and gives lectures on crime issues. It also helps residents to security mark their property so it can be returned if found after a burglary. The NYPD organises a variety of programmes to help stop car and bike theft within the city and provides a range of crime prevention literature.

New York Police Department Statistics for 2004

|  | Reported cases | % change since 1993 |
|---|---|---|
| Murder | 572 | -70.3 |
| Rape | 1 741 | -46 |
| Robbery | 24 124 | -71.9 |
| Assault | 18 186 | -55.7 |
| Burglary | 26 815 | -73.4 |
| Theft | 48 361 | -43.5 |
| Car theft | 20 288 | -81.8 |

◀ Tourist areas are policed by foot patrols.

# The New York economy

Unemployment levels are low in New York City – in 2005 the rate was 5.3 per cent. However, many jobs are in the service sector and these may be low paid.

Poorer New Yorkers may have to hold down two jobs to be able to survive in the city. Although today most of New York's residents are employed within the services sector (including jobs in education, finance, retailing, transportation and administration), this has been a relatively recent change. The city grew on trade with Europe and beyond – an early example of globalisation – and many of its early industries were based on the goods that went through the port, such as sugar refining. Later in the nineteenth century there were heavy industries, such as metal working and other forms of manufacturing. At the same time as these

industries were thriving, service industries such as banking and finance were developing to support them. These industries now dominate New York's economy. Manufacturing industries have largely moved over the Hudson River into the state of New Jersey or out to the suburbs where there is room for modern factories and the land is cheaper. The southern end of Manhattan, which was once an important area for manufacturing and port industries, is now the main financial district of the city. It can be recognised by the clustering of very tall skyscrapers. Some old industries such as garment manufacture have managed to remain in Manhattan, even though the original reasons for the location have disappeared. The area has a skilled labour force and a successful fashion industry has developed there now.

▲ Skilled workers continue to make clothing in the Garment District, in Manhattan, for the fashion industry.

▶ Major fashion brands based in New York include Donna Karan, Marc Jacobs and Ralph Lauren. This fashion designer works as one of a team of designers at Donna Karan, a major label that was started in New York in 1984, based in the Garment District.

Primary Industry 4.4%

Manufacturing 6.6%

Services
89%

▲ Areas of employment in New York City (%)

# Fulton Fish Market

The Fulton Fish Market was founded in 1821 and was located in Manhattan, near the South Street Seaport. It was a popular sight for visitors, and local people enjoyed being able to buy freshly-caught fish every morning. Even though the market was near to the port, fish no longer comes in directly from boats but by truck from fishing quays elsewhere. It is difficult to drive delivery trucks across Manhattan because of traffic congestion, so the market will be moving out to Hunts Point in the Bronx. Although not a popular move with traditionalists, it has meant that road and rail access is much better and the market is in a purpose-built facility that meets modern high safety and hygiene standards.

◀ Most of the fish in Fulton Fish Market is sold before dawn!

## CASE STUDY

### Anthony Bencivenga, fish wholesaler

Anthony is 62 years old and is one of the longest-working fishmongers in the Fulton Street Market. He began work at 14 and now employs 40 people, importing fish from all over the world. He lives outside the city where it is quieter and is looking forward to moving his business to Hunts Point. "At Fulton Street this is no way to run a multi-million dollar-industry. Nothing has changed here for 200 years. The move to Hunts Point will cost us more but it's clean, spacious and above all it's environmentally hygienic."

# Banking and finance

New York City is the financial centre of the USA, and one of the three biggest financial centres in the global economy. The New York Stock Exchange and headquarters of many national banks and insurance companies are located in the Financial District around Wall Street in southern Manhattan, near the Hudson River. The Stock Exchange is one of the busiest and most eagerly-watched in the world, with the shares of over 2000 companies being traded. Having such an important financial centre attracts other businesses to the city, as they want to be close to the place where decisions are made.

▶ The statue of George Washington, standing in front of the Federal Hall, looks towards the front of the New York Stock Exchange, in the heart of the Financial District.

# Advertising and the media

Many advertising firms are located in New York to be close to the great range of businesses that require their services. Some of these advertising firms will be small web-based ones, but others provide the advertising needed by large international companies. Being located in an appealing and exciting city also attracts young advertising executives with new ideas to use to market products.

There are many large book publishers located in New York, including Scholastic – the largest publisher and distributor of children's books in the USA. There are also several national newspapers produced in

the city including the *Wall Street Journal*, which is a daily financial publication, and the prestigious *New York Times*. A range of magazines are produced, including *Newsweek*, a weekly summary of national and international news.

With more than 145 studios and stages in the city, New York is becoming ever more popular as a film or TV location, rivalling the huge industry of Los Angeles. Films and programmes made in the city are shown around the world. There are many local drama schools and colleges of performing arts that provide a steady supply of young actors looking for work.

▲ Times Square, in central Manhattan, is famous for its brightly-lit advertising.

## CASE STUDY

### Lisa Gallagher, Publisher

Lisa is Publisher of William Morrow, part of Harper Collins in New York. New York is the hub of book publishing in the United States, with hundreds of publishing companies of all sizes employing tens of thousands of people. Lisa, who has worked in publishing in New York since 1998, says, "Being in New York puts a publisher at the centre of the dynamic artistic and cultural capital of the country, which helps us to produce the books we think will appeal to the reading public."

## High-tech industries

There are over 4,000 technology and media companies in New York. Originally most of these firms were located in the south of Manhattan. Over the last ten years these firms, including telecommunications and information technology companies, have moved to northern Manhattan, Queens and Brooklyn. The firms want to locate in New York for the easy access to possible investors, and to be close to world-class universities, their research departments and a pool of well-qualified young graduates. High-technology firms also tend to cluster together, as this allows an exchange of ideas and faster development. The city location helps firms keep their workers as it offers a potentially better quality of life. The state of New York wants to encourage high-tech industries as they are providing a range of new jobs.

31

▲ Tourists, here on a sight-seeing tour, provide an important part of the city's income.

# Tourism

Tourism is a very important service industry for New York. In 2004 there were 40 million visitors to the city. Whilst there they spent over US$15 billion and through their spending supported over a quarter of a million jobs. These service jobs include city guides, hotel workers, tour operators and tour bus drivers. The people employed had money to spend within the city economy, too, further contributing to the city. Now that air travel is cheaper, New York is no longer the once-in-a-lifetime long-haul destination it once was. People may now visit the city from Europe for a few days just to do their Christmas shopping or to visit the sales in the big department stores. Although temperatures can be freezing in winter there is much to see that is under cover and New York is now an all-year-round destination.

# Marketing the city

NYC & Company is New York's official tourism marketing organisation. It provides information and assistance to business and tourists via the web, pamphlets and by advertising in various journals. It also helps to publicise activities to help the many tourist-dependent firms get as many people as possible to come to stay in and enjoy the city – and spend lots of money!

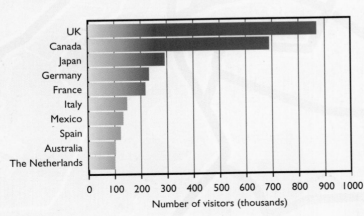

◀ The top ten countries providing international tourist visitors to New York (2003).

# A safe destination

As its crime rates have seen a steady and significant reduction since 1993, New York is now the safest of the large cities of the USA. Daytime travel on public transport is viewed as safe and cheap, and is used by large numbers of tourists.

New York wants to continue to increase its numbers of visitors, especially from overseas. One initiative the city has helped organise is CultureFest, a showcase of arts and cultural organisations which now occurs annually in Battery Park, right at the southern tip of Manhattan.

▶ The entrance lobby of the Empire State Building, perhaps New York's most famous building. Tourists can ascend to the top of the building to take in the famous Manhattan skyline.

▼ A horse-drawn carriage taking visitors on a leisurely tour of Central Park.

# Regeneration

Once industry or activity moves out of an area, there is often a need to restore and redevelop the locality so that it can be sustained as a productive area. It may be changed into a residential area, an area of light industry, a tourist site, an area of green space or a mix of all these. Land that is left derelict is transformed to the benefit of the local community.

# South Street Seaport

This is a waterfront area in the south east of Manhattan, and was the heart of the nineteenth century port. When sailing ships dominated, it was a bustling area of warehouses and inns and South Street was known as "The Street of Ships". However, during the second half of the nineteenth century this port area began to decline as heavier and larger steam ships needed the deeper water found on the west side of Manhattan on the Hudson River. By the mid-twentieth century the area only had the Fulton Fish Market remaining of its port industries and was looking very run down. During the 1960s it was decided to restore and redevelop the area. Part of the

▲ Buildings in the South Street Seaport area awaiting redevelopment.

seaport area has been pedestrianised so that visitors can escape from the usual New York traffic. The historic buildings now house restaurants, craft shops and the South Street Seaport Museum. Pier 17 was redeveloped in 1982 and now has a pavilion made of glass and steel. This has three floors and there are shops, food stalls and restaurants. The top floor has views of the Brooklyn Bridge and the New York harbour. Visitors now come for the views, to eat and to enjoy the craft demonstrations and shops. Workers from the nearby Financial District lunch here on a daily basis and the port has become a lively area once again.

◄ The South Street Seaport has been restored to provide a range of retail and eating outlets, and is popular with locals.

▲ East River Harbour in the South Street Seaport looking towards lower Manhattan.

# Brooklyn waterfront

Although there is still some maritime use of the Brooklyn waterfront, much of the area has derelict buildings, such as old sugar refineries and warehouses. The Brooklyn Navy Yard, which closed in 1966, has started to be redeveloped. It is a large site with good views over to Manhattan. One of the first developments was Steiner Studios, which opened in 2004. The studios have stages, offices and dressing rooms, plus a 100-seat room for showing films. Light industries and offices are being attracted into the secure Navy site.

Other developments planned for Brooklyn include building over the railyards. This aims to create a community in a previously run-down area by building a mixed use area, including a sports stadium, blocks of low and middle income housing, open recreation space, and offices.

# Managing New York

Although New York City is in New York State and comes under that State's laws, it has considerable powers of its own through its City Council.

▲ City Hall, built in the early nineteenth century, is the seat of government for New York City.

The government of the city has three branches: executive (overseeing of departments that run the day-to-day activities of the city); legislative (creating laws for the city); and judicial (the work of the civil court of the city). The City Council is made up of 51 members from the 51 Council Districts that make up the City of New York. Each member represents the views of about 157,000 people. It is the Council that can make laws for the city and it decides how much can be spent and on what within the city. The Council checks how various city departments are performing, and its members sit on committees linked to the departments.

The head of the Council is the Speaker, who is elected by the council members. His main job is to get an overall agreement on major issues from Council members. The government of New York is led by the mayor, who is elected by the citizens of the City every four years. In 2005 Michael Bloomberg became the 108th Mayor of New York. He is aided by five deputy mayors. The Mayor has to approve decisions made by the council. If he disagrees with a decision the matter is returned to the council for reconsideration. However, if it then receives a clear majority, the Council can override the Mayor's decision.

# Departments

There are a number of departments covering areas such as transport and parks. These departments carry out the work needed and approved by the City Council. The Department of Environmental Protection has more than 5,700 people working for it. It protects water courses from pollution, ensures a good quality drinking water supply and aims to improve air quality. The Department of Youth and Community Affairs provides information for youth and community groups, funds some work experience and youth activities and develops programmes of youth work.

▶ The Department of Health battles the city's rat infestation.

▲ Much of the city's waste goes to landfill sites in other states.

◀ City traffic officers are needed to keep the traffic moving.

# Committees

Each Council member usually sits on about three committees which oversee the various functions of city government. The results of committee meetings can be accessed on-line so New York citizens can see what is taking place within their government.

# The Department of City Planning

This important department is responsible for making decisions about how land can be used or developed. It controls the zoning of land use so that, for example, industrial zones are kept separate from residential areas. City Planning has to resolve conflicts between the often competing uses of industrial, residential and transport land uses, as well as planning for recreational space. They aim to ensure that any growth is sustainable and improves the landscapes of the city for all its citizens.

▲ A view of Manhattan showing the density of building on the island. New developments must be tightly controlled.

# Planning conflicts

Throgs Neck is an area by the water in the Bronx where there is conflict between the residents and developers. The residents feel that the character of the area is being changed by the inappropriate development of tall, multi-family town houses along the waterfront. There was also a problem with a lack of car parking for residents. The Planning Department have resolved the problem by re-zoning Throgs Neck as a Lower Density Growth Management (LDGM) area. This gives priority to single-family houses built at a low density – houses with front, side and back gardens.

New houses on the waterfront cannot be more than two stories high so they do not restrict views to the water, and there must be spaces between the individual houses. Widths of building plots have also been increased so that cars can be parked within the property boundary and not affect the character of the area. New waterfront houses must also have gardens to the front to improve the appearance of the area from the water. Re-zoning has ensured that landowners know the rules set out by the Planning Department for any future developments.

# Hudson Yards

As part of the development of the west side of Manhattan, the area known as Hudson Yards is to provide an extension of the island's central business area. The increased pressure of urbanisation, as more companies locate their headquarters in New York, and as more workers are attracted to live in the city, means there is a need for more building of office and residential space. This will help stop the movement out of the city to find adequate office space and will slow down urbanisation at the edge of the city.

Hudson Yards is a 150-hectare area, part of which has railway lines and yards on it. The Planning Department's ideas for the future include covering the railyards and allowing building on top. By 2012 the subway link and basic clearance would be completed. Private developers would then move in to build offices and homes.

▲ The under-used area around the Hudson Railyards is to be redeveloped to provide much needed office and living space for west Manhattan.

## CASE STUDY

# Ryan Singer – city planner

Ryan came to New York from Seattle three years ago to work as a city planner. The city is changing so fast that it needs a long-term outlook. "Our job in the Planning Department is one of balancing the needs of developers and businesses who want to expand and residents who wish to live in a better environment. Environmental issues are important as too many apartment blocks lead to more cars and then more air pollution. We are aiming to build on more brownfield sites to reuse land in the city. Keeping new residential properties out of the sky – that is more high density, low-rise buildings – should lead to a cleaner and friendlier neighbourhood for all of us – just like the old days!"

# Transport for New York

When New York was first settled it was a compact town, and people either walked or used horse-drawn transport such as carriages or carts. Gradually the island of Manhattan became too crowded and people settled the other boroughs. They could not live very far away as commuting at the speed of a horse was slow. From the beginning of the twentieth century other types of transport became possible and people could live much further out. This led to increasing urban sprawl.

▲ Looking across Manhattan Bridge (foreground) and Brooklyn Bridge (rear) towards the borough of Brooklyn.

## City centre problems

As Manhattan is an island, efficient transport links have always been important. Today the island is linked to the other boroughs by 17 main bridges and four tunnels. The most famous bridge link is the Brooklyn Bridge, built in 1883, which links Brooklyn to Manhattan. During peak times the bridge and tunnel links become very congested with car and lorry traffic. In 2002 it was calculated that the average time spent commuting to work in a year by New Yorkers was 6.7 days, compared with 4.9 for Los Angeles. The City's government is trying, through a number of different initiatives, to reduce the number of cars entering the centre to improve both traffic flow and air quality.

▼ Heavy Manhattan-bound rush-hour traffic.

# Railway and subway

Above-ground rail access to Manhattan is limited. Commuter trains come into Grand Central Station from the suburbs to the north and east, and long distance trains come into Pennsylvania Station. In 1904 the subway opened. Today there are 480 subway stations in the city. In 2002 4.8 million passengers were carried per day by subway, but the system is in need of

▲ Grand Central Station is an important rail hub and popular tourist destination.

updating. Recently carriages have been introduced which are computer-aided and give passengers updated information about arrival times. They are far more technologically-advanced than the old carriages, and with the energy created by braking being fed back into the power system they are also more environmentally-friendly.

▲ A section of the now disused elevated railway.

# The elevated railway

In the 1930s the railway was raised above the road level to help avoid accidents and to save having level crossings. This was the elevated railway, known affectionately as 'the El'. Trains stopped running on it in 1980 and the railway was allowed to become derelict and covered in wild flowers. However, part of the El in the West Side of Manhattan,

called the High Line, is about to be restored into a green walkway, a sort of promenade above the street linking in to the general development of that side of Manhattan. It will mean that people can walk for 22 blocks without using roads and have access to the waterfront regeneration area too.

# Taking the bus

Buses began to carry passengers in the city in 1907. Today there are over 200 local routes and 4,500 buses within New York. The city is moving towards greener, more sustainable transport, and now has over 6,000 buses running on alternative fuels such as Compressed Natural Gas (CNG), electricity and bio-fuel (a fuel made from plants). Some buses run on a mixture of low sulphur diesel and electric motors. The two combine to give economical running with far lower emissions than standard buses. The aim of the City's Department of Transport is to provide New Yorkers with an efficient service while at the same time improving air quality.

▲ Many of the city's 4,500 blue and white buses run on a 24-hour schedule.

◀ ▼ The subway is the quickest way to travel around the centre of New York, but it can become very crowded at peak times.

# Airports

New York has three airports. The main international airport is the John F. Kennedy (JFK) which is in Brooklyn, about 25 km away from Manhattan. In 2002 it dealt with 35 million passengers. The second international airport is Newark Liberty International which is only 17 km away in New Jersey. It has easy access to Manhattan by train but people think it is further away as it is in the next state, just over the Hudson River. The third airport is La Guardia which is 14 km away from Manhattan in the borough of Queens. This is mainly a domestic airport as it cannot take wide-bodied jets. The links between the airports and the centre of the city have been improved, with dedicated train and bus services offering a fast and reasonably priced alternative to driving and parking a car. It also has the impact of reducing traffic congestion and exhaust emissions on the approach roads.

# Shipping

Sometimes it is difficult to remember that New York is still an important port. Although much of the commercial shipping has moved across the Hudson to better sites in New Jersey (but still remains part of the Port of New York), Manhattan is an important port of call for cruise liners. The New York Cruise Terminal is being upgraded to cope with the increasing number of visitors who arrive in the city by ship. A new cruise terminal is also being developed in Brooklyn, the first part of which opened in 2005. Ferries are an everyday feature of the harbour. The most famous is the free service from Manhattan to Staten Island which is heavily used by both commuters and tourists. There are many others whose existence allows commuters to leave their cars outside the central city.

▼ The free Staten Island ferry runs to and from Manhattan 24 hours a day.

## CASE STUDY

## Charlie Ventycinque – taxi driver

Charlie came from Italy with his parents when he was eight, and has never returned. He works as a taxi driver on Staten Island. "Life on Staten Island is fine. I'd hate to have to deal with the rush and push over on Manhattan. I avoid going there like the plague. Now the new ferry terminal has been built there are even more commuters living over here and working in the city. It's safer living over here and if they can afford the property prices – good luck to them. It means more business for me too!"

# Culture, leisure and tourism

New York has an enormous range of cultural and leisure attractions, with world-famous museums, art galleries, theatres and a glittering and energetic nightlife. It has a huge range of parks and open spaces.

## Central Park

The most famous of all of the city's parks is Central Park in Manhattan. It was planned in 1858 to be the backyard (or garden) for all New Yorkers without access to their own green space. The 340-hectare site was previously a mixture of swamps, piggeries and quarries but today is a magnificent open space with lakes, hills and meadows. It has roads across it but cars are banned at weekends to make the area safer and more pleasant. On a summer's day thousands of New Yorkers

▲ A popular spot for children within Central Park, this scene from Alice in Wonderland is made of bronze.

can be seen enjoying the sun in the open glades or sitting by the more formal gardens. There are also basketball and volleyball courts for hire and they are well used. On the paths around the park are joggers and many roller bladers but probably the best way to see this huge park is to hire a bicycle.

▲ In the heat of the summer Central Park offers shaded paths for those walking or just sitting on a bench.

## Other open spaces

Other parks are dotted all over the city, giving the residents the chance for a view of sky and some greenery. Battery Park is located at the southern end of Manhattan and gives excellent views of the ocean. There are other parks around the edge of Manhattan as well as some smaller ones within it. The present mayor of New York,

Michael Bloomberg, has stated that he would like to see a recreational path around all of Manhattan for the use of residents for walking, playing or generally relaxing. Prospect Park, Brooklyn, is another large park created in the nineteenth century to offer recreational space to residents who lived in the new suburbs.

The Bronx is home to both the world-class Bronx Zoo and to the New York Botanical Gardens. The zoo specialises in the breeding of endangered species such as the lowland gorilla and has created exhibits that do away with traditional cages and bars. Moats, deep ditches, and glass are used to separate people and animals. This is a popular day out for New Yorkers, especially on Wednesdays when entry is via voluntary donation. The Botanical Gardens were created at the end of the nineteenth century and are set in 101 hectares. The huge glasshouses have desert and tropical habitats within them.

▶ A gorilla in the Bronx Zoo.

## CASE STUDY

# Bingo Wyer – Central Park volunteer

Bingo works as a writer and journalist for New York-based papers and magazines but in her spare time works as a volunteer in Central Park. "I've worked as a volunteer in Central Park for just two months. We work in small groups of about ten people, clearing leaves or pruning back trees and bushes – generally making the place tidy. We operate under the supervision of a paid Park Ranger who works full time for the New York Parks Service. The volunteers have been going for 25 years and it's just one more way we New Yorkers can put a little back into our own community and make our Central Park even more special."

# The theatre and the arts

New York offers residents and visitors alike a huge range of venues for theatre, concerts and dance. In 1833 the Metropolitan Opera House moved to Broadway. This encouraged other theatres, restaurants and hotels to locate there. Today, the Theatre District is still located in this area, with well-known plays being 'on Broadway' and those less well-known or more experimental appearing 'off Broadway'. Later, with the advent of film, large cinemas were developed in the same area. By the 1920s there were so many neon lights outside the various Broadway venues that the street became known as the "Great White Way". Times Square is at the heart of the Theater District and many visitors go to the Square just to look at all the neon lights of the theatres and advertisers. There are the traditional theatres but also a range of other venues such as the Performing Garage, where visitors can see experimental theatre.

Shakespeare in the Park is a summer event when plays are performed in the open air in Central Park. Alternatively there is Shakespeare in the Park(ing Lot), another free event but taking place in a city car park in Manhattan! New York has five ballet companies as well as many venues for seeing contemporary dance. The Brooklyn Academy of Music is an important dance venue and hosts the annual DanceAfrica Festival.

Carnegie Hall is the world famous concert hall located in the Theatre District. It hosts important orchestras from around the world. Once home to the New York Philharmonic Orchestra, they now play at the Avery Fisher Hall, but give free concerts in Central Park during the summer. These are very popular and many thousands of New Yorkers attend.

▼ Broadway is at the heart of New York's theatre district and offers a wide variety of entertainment.

# Museums and galleries

New York is home to many important art galleries and museums as well as to smaller, specialised collections. There are more than 60 museums in Manhattan alone. The Museum of Modern Art (MoMA) houses one of the largest and most important collections of modern art in the world. It shows paintings, sculpture, books, film and design. Another museum containing modern art is the Guggenheim Museum. It is not just the collection that is important, but also the building that contains it, which was designed by the architect Frank Lloyd Wright. It has a curving shape which contrasts with the usual straight-sided skyscrapers of the city.

Other museums display furniture, older art collections, personal art collections, history and natural history. The Museum of the American Indian covers the history and

▲ Art collections like the Guggenheim (above) and The Museum of the Native American (lower image) attract large numbers of visitors.

culture of native Americans and houses over a million artefacts. New York residents and visitors have access to one of the largest ranges of cultural activity in the world. The many free concerts and plays allow all the cities residents to enjoy cultural events, regardless of their incomes.

# Getting outside

Participating in and watching sport is integral to lots of New Yorker's lives. They have several good teams in a variety of sports, including baseball, basketball and American football. Although not everyone participates in a sport, watching the professionals is an extremely popular activity. This can be by attending a game, watching on television at home or with others in the sports bars which have giant screens to show popular games.

Baseball matches are often attended by families and are the best value for money. The Yankee Stadium in the Bronx is home to the New York Yankees, a top baseball team. It is rare for there to be any violence or misbehaviour at these matches and they are suitable entertainment for all members of the family. The Knicks are an important basketball team and play most of their matches at Madison Square Gardens, a large sports and entertainment venue

▲ Jogging is a popular way of keeping fit in many of New York's parks.

seating up to 20,000 people. This location is also home to the New York Rangers, the top ice hockey team. Other sports include jogging, for which the most popular location is around the Reservoir in Central Park. Cycling is also popular in parks such as Central, Riverside and the East River Park and there are over 100 km of cycle paths in the city. Croquet and chess can be played in Central Park. Cafés may also offer chess, although in Chinatown this might be replaced by games of mah-jong. Apart from official sporting venues there are derelict sites where local youths play football, baseball or create their own cycle tracks. Skateboarding is a popular pastime and the city's newly pedestrianised areas provide ideal locations for youths to practise their skills – a decision that is not always popular with the authorities or other local residents.

◀ Young people often socialise through playing sport. Basketball is particularly popular.

# At the beach

A day at the beach is easily reached from central New York by taking the subway out to Coney Island in Brooklyn. There are fairground rides and amusements alongside the wide beaches that face the Atlantic.

It can be crowded in the summer when people come in large numbers to escape the heat and stifling humidity of the city.

▼ The wide beaches and pleasant sand make the Coney Island beach a popular weekend destination.

# The New York environment

Like all large cities, New York has to cope with an environment constantly strained by the over-use of resources and an ever-growing demand for the removal of waste products. New and creative responses to the demands of a growing population constantly need to be found to keep the city sustainable.

## A thirsty city

When the city of New York was first settled the water supply came from shallow wells dug in Manhattan, but as the population increased there was a need to store water in order to have a continual supply. The first reservoir was built in 1776 when the city's population was about 22,000. By the middle of the nineteenth century it was realised that much more water was needed and so the Croton River to the north of New York was dammed. Aqueducts brought water into the city, and by the early twentieth century water was also being brought in from the Catskill and Delaware rivers, to the west of the city. Today there are 19 reservoirs and three

▼ New York draws much of its water from rivers and lakes to the west of the city.

controlled lakes providing water plus some water pumped from aquifers (water-bearing rocks) in Queens and Brooklyn. 90 per cent of today's water comes from the Catskill/Delaware rivers, with just under 10 per cent from the Croton River. The water from the aquifer only provides about 1 per cent of the water supply.

# Water use in the city

The water supply system provides New Yorkers with 5.5 billion litres of clean drinking water every day, 2008 billion litres a year. The Department of Environmental Protection (DEP) is responsible for the water supply and has to maintain the kilometres of mains, tunnels and the two largest underground storage tanks in the world. They use sonar (echo sounding) equipment to help them detect leaks in the pipes – it is otherwise difficult to trace them underneath roads and pavements. The DEP also encourages people to be less wasteful with their water use and places limitations on some uses such as watering lawns. At present the city is constructing a huge new water tunnel, City Water Tunnel Number 3, to improve water delivery.

# Waste water

New York has 14 waste water treatment plants, which require constant monitoring and maintenance. Water comes from domestic and industrial uses, plus water from storm drainage. Sewage sludge is the solid waste left at the treatment plant after the processing of all the waste water. Until 1992 this was taken by barge and dumped in the ocean 20 km offshore. Now much is taken out of the state and sprayed onto land as a fertiliser, composted, or placed in landfill sites. In some areas, such as the South Shore of Staten Island, a bluebelt system is used to treat some storm waste water. Here, by allowing streams, ponds and wetlands to carry out their natural functions of carrying water, storing it and filtering it through reeds, the city saves on costs and provides a natural landscape. There are 16 systems in place and others are planned. This is a more sustainable way of dealing with waste water.

▼ One of the reservoirs from which New York takes its water.

# Garbage disposal

In 2005 the residents, schools and hospitals of New York City produced over 61,500 tonnes of rubbish every week; this is more than three million tonnes a year. In addition that year two million tonnes of waste for recycling was collected. In contrast the whole of the United Kingdom produces 35 million tonnes a year. On top of all this there is also 13,000 tonnes of rubbish generated daily by commercial sources, but their waste is collected by private companies. This is a gigantic amount of waste for any city to have to deal with, and a serious problem if New York is to be sustainable. The DOS employs nearly 7,000 people and has a huge fleet of vehicles dedicated to keeping the city clean.

There are up to three rubbish collections a week in most areas. While much of the waste produced is recycled, this is less than other cities of a comparable size, such as Los Angeles, which recycles about 40 per cent. Until 2001 rubbish was taken by barge to Fresh Kills on Staten Island (see p. 53) to be put into a huge landfill site. Now that site is closed, the rubbish is taken to landfill sites in other states, some as far as 500 km away. Although some of the rubbish could be incinerated (burned) it would produce too many harmful gases and toxins. New Yorkers are being encouraged to "Reduce, Reuse and Recycle", but there is much work to be done in reducing waste.

▼ If rubbish is not collected quickly it attracts rats and other vermin, causing a possible health hazard.

# The Fresh Kills landfill

The landfill site at Fresh Kills opened in 1948 on an 890 hectare area of open land and wetlands. It took in thousands of tonnes of mainly domestic rubbish a day, forming four huge mounds, one as tall as the Statue of Liberty. The landfill site is so large it can be seen from space! The site was unlined, so over time thousands of litres of toxic wastes have leached into the local water courses. Eventually it was realised that the landfill was badly affecting the environment of Staten Island and the site was closed. It had to re-open briefly to take the debris from the destruction of the World Trade Center. This debris was carefully sorted on site to check for human remains. Part of the plans for the area include a memorial to those who died. Now that Fresh Kills is fully closed as a landfill site plans are underway to turn it into a large-scale park. The wetland areas are to be preserved and the waste mounds are to be landscaped to create an attractive recreational area with access to rivers and the sea.

▼ Posters encourage New Yorkers to recycle most types of waste in order to reduce disposal costs.

▼ Huge amounts of cardboard used in shops in the city are now recycled.

## Caring for the environment

New Yorkers are becoming more aware of their impact on the environment. Many realise that individuals need to make changes to their lifestyles in order to limit their impact on the city's environments. There are several groups working to help build community gardens on derelict sites, and others that organise the recycling of kitchen and garden waste. The New York Restoration Project was started in 1995 by the actress Bette Midler, with the aim of developing small derelict areas into communal gardens. Such gardens can help a neighbourhood to work together and in many cases petty vandalism is reduced. When local people are involved in creating a garden it tends to be well looked after as they feel a sense of ownership.

▲ The Adopt-a-Highway scheme encourages local organisations and firms to undertake regular litter removal along a certain stretch of road, in return for the publicity when their name is put up by the road.

▼ Community gardens improve the local environment for everyone, providing green spaces in many crowded areas of the city.

In a large city like New York it is not always easy to recycle organic material, such as kitchen or garden wastes. In the Lower East Side of Manhattan individual residents are able to send their compostable waste to the Compost Education Centre. The centre accepts organic waste from local residents, then turns it into compost which can then be sold to local gardeners to cover costs. In the future similar methods will become more necessary as the city aims to reduce the amount of waste it has to remove.

## Jamaica Bay

This area of 5,500 hectares of wetlands lies on the southern shores of Brooklyn, near to JFK Airport. Until the late twentieth century it was used as a landfill and parts were drained and used for commercial development. It was largely ignored as an area of open recreational space. Three quarters of the wetlands area is now gone, but what is left is important for migrating birds and as a general wetland habitat. "Friends of the Bay" is an organisation that fights to protect this landscape. The area is now known as the Jamaica Bay Wildlife Refuge Centre and is part of the Gateway National Recreation Area. An open and wild landscape, it is only a subway ride away from Manhattan and many New Yorkers take advantage of the location to get closer to nature.

▼ The Jamaica Bay wetlands, off Brooklyn.

## CASE STUDY

## Sally Young – garden organiser

Sally helps organise the community garden at the 6th and B (a junction of two roads). Community gardens help people to come together to work for a common cause. "There are hundreds of community gardens all over New York using unused or derelict land. Some are pretty organised like ours with members and committees, others are simple little plots on waste ground. But we're all doing our bit for biodiversity in a city most known for its streets, traffic horrors and its night life. We have all worked so hard to make this the place you see today – a tiny haven for people and wildlife, especially butterflies, amid the noise and bustle of a huge city. Each member has a little plot and can grow whatever they like, flowers, vegetables or even nurturing the wild plants that spring up on their own."

# The New York of tomorrow

New York is a large city and it is difficult for it to be truly sustainable. New York has to import large amounts of water, food and energy into its boundaries and the area it needs to draw on in order to have these essentials is vast. However, New York is working on reducing its resource demands.

In the future there will need to be larger numbers of the fuel efficient buses and subways, but more will have to be done to reduce car use in the city centre. New zoning measures help to protect public health by separating industrial and residential uses. There are more residential developments in the city centre, encouraging young professionals back into areas abandoned in previous decades. Living near to their place of work is a more sustainable option and means less car use. As fossil fuels run out people may not have the choice of being able to commute long distances to work. New York plans to attract new industries in the future by helping to fund Science Parks today, where new ideas may lead to more high-tech jobs for the city.

Recycling of wastes continues to be encouraged but some feel that in the future there should be a tax on all throwaway products such as plastic cups. This would help fund waste disposal, although it would be far better to make everything recyclable or reusable. Green space will continue to have importance in all planned developments but also at a local level where people work together to

▼ Onlookers reading about the events at Ground Zero, the site of the destruction of the World Trade Center. A new tower will be built on the site.

▲ A film crew filming an event highlighting the use of cleaner fuels in New York taxis, helping to improve the air quality of the city.

produce community gardens. The future will see the completion of the greening of the city's waterfront edges and the opening of the Elevated Railway track (see page 41) as a green walkway.

Reduced car use, less waste, more greenery and better air quality are achievable goals for the city, but they will not be easy, and will require changes not only in the way the city is run, but also in the way that the people of the city view the importance of good citizenship.

▶ Kids on the block. "New York is a great place to live and we can't think of spending our lives anyplace else."

# Glossary

**Aquifer** A layer of porous rock that holds water.

**Biodiversity** The variety of species found within an area.

**Birth Rate** The number of births per thousand population, usually expressed as a percentage.

**Brownfield Site** A site that has already been used in the past which is now available for redevelopment.

**Brownstone houses** Houses built in the nineteenth century from the local brown sandstone.

**Death Rate** The number of deaths per thousand population, usually expressed as a percentage.

**Depression, the Great** A period that began in 1929 with the Stock Market crash. There were huge job losses and people lost a lot of money. It lasted until the beginning of World War Two.

**Emigrant** A person who leaves their country of birth to live and work in another country.

**Gentrification** This is when an inner city area that was home to low income groups is moved into by people on higher incomes. They then upgrade the houses and the area changes character.

**High Tech Industries** Industries that use the latest production techniques and technology.

**Hispanic** Someone from Spanish-speaking countries such as Mexico or Honduras.

**Migrant** A general term for a person who moves area for work or education.

**Multicultural** The presence of many racial groups, nationalities and cultures.

**Pedestrianisation** The closing of a street or an area to traffic, making it easier for people on foot.

**Primary Industry** This is any extractive industry and includes mining, agriculture, forestry, fishing and quarrying.

**Retailing** This is the service industry involved in the selling of goods.

**Regeneration (urban)** This is when decision makers such as city councils, try to improve a run down area. Money is used to create a better living and working environment so that businesses are attracted in to the area and help drive its recovery forward.

**Reservoir** An artificially created storage lake for holding water supply.

**Secondary Industry** Industries that use raw materials to manufacture goods.

**Service Industry** (Sometimes called Tertiary Industry). Industries that provide services for people and companies such as taxis, banks and shops.

**Suburbs** The outer areas of a city where housing dominates.

**Suburbanisation** The process by which people move out from the city centre to live in the outer areas but often returning to the centre for work and entertainment.

**Subway** The underground railway system of New York.

**Tenement Building** These are early blocks of flats to house those on low incomes in the nineteenth century. Few remain as they were poorly planned, crowded and with little ventilation.

**Urbanisation** This is the movement of people from rural to urban areas.

**Urban Sprawl** This is when towns and cities grow outwards in an unplanned way. One or more cities may join together to form a conurbation.

# Further information

## Useful websites

http:/www./nyc.gov/portal/index.jsp?front_door=true

The website for New York City Council. It has many links to different departments as well as a useful Frequently Asked Questions page. The Department of Planning can easily be accessed so you can see new plans for the city.

http://www.nycvisit.com/home/index.cfm

This is the website for New York and Company, the marketing company for the city which has much up-to-date information about what is happening in New York.

## Books

### Non-fiction

*Eyewitness Travel Guides - New York* (Dorling Kindersley) Updated annually.
Highly illustrated book of information on the city. Some history and cultural background plus background information on the major, and many minor, sights.

*The Mini Rough Guide to New York City* by Martin Dunford and Jack Holland (Rough Guides, 2002).
Much more a guide for visitors but gives up-to-date information about what is going on in the city that would appeal to young people.

*The Brit's Guide to New York* by Karen Marchbank (Foulsham, 2004) Upbeat guide to all that's good about New York.

*Countries of the World USA* by Sally Garrington (Evans, 2002) Background to the country as a whole, including its large cities.

### Fiction

*It's Like This, Cat* by Emily Cheney Neville (Harper Trophy, 1992).
Set in the 1960s and includes locations such as Coney Beach.

*All-of-a-Kind Family* by Sydney Taylor, (Bantam Doubleday Dell Publishing Inc., 1996).
Although written for a younger audience all ages can enjoy this story set in early twentieth century New York. It deals with the lives of the daughters of a Jewish family and includes many references to New York locations and to Jewish culture.

# Index

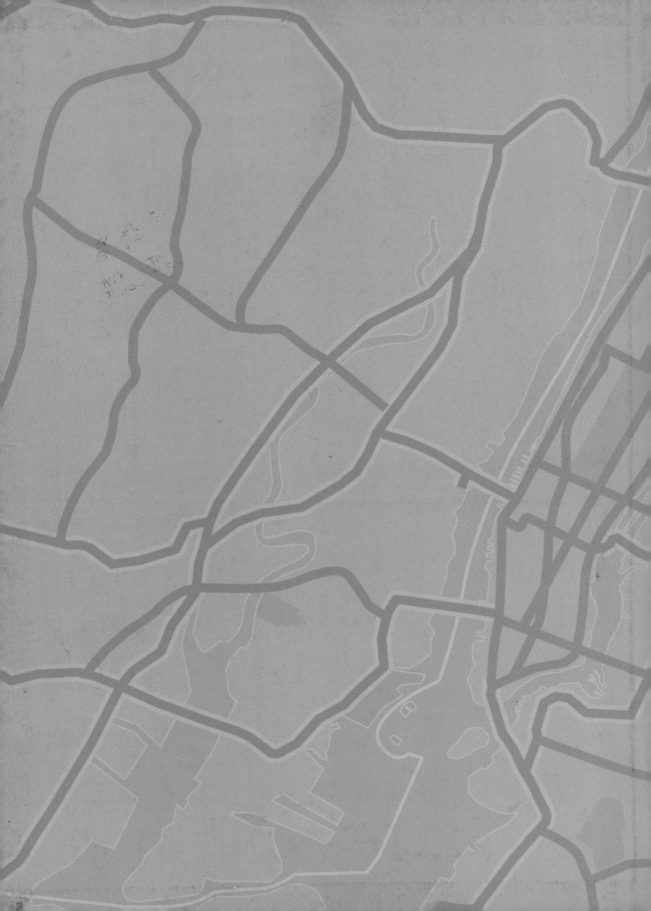